I0411329

Wind Energy Essentials for the Homeowner

Common Questions about Wind Energy for the Home

Blake Webster

Copyright © 2013 by Blake Webster

All rights reserved. No part of this book may be reproduced or transmitted in any form or by any means, electronic or mechanical, including photocopying, recording, or by any information storage and retrieval system, without permission in writing from the copyright owner.

Books by Blake Webster

Solar Energy Essentials for the Homeowner

How to Make Money Writing for the Internet

How to Self-Publish Your Book the CreateSpace Way

How to Start Your Online Photography Store

Greener Living Today: Forty Ways to a Greener Lifestyle

How to Start Your Online Affiliate Store: Step-by-Step Guide to Making Money Online

Environmentalists in Action: Profiles of Green Pioneers

Table of Contents

What are the Pros and Cons of Wind Energy?

One of the key benefits to using wind as energy is that it is useful and inexpensive. The cost to implement windmills can often be cheaper compared to adapting solar panels to ones existing grid, thus making it an option for both the wealthy and the poor. Depending on the geographical location of the windmill, low income families or farmers could actually earn a second stream of income from the housing of a windmill by providing electricity to themselves as well as other homes nearby.

Unlike converting solar rays into energy, wind can be prevalent during both the day and the night. Studies indicate that wind is a never-ending resource, therefore power cuts and power failures are almost non-existent in areas that rely upon wind power to generate electricity.

Fortunately for the overall good, as wind is transformed into energy it does not involve the use of any fossil fuels or non-renewable sources of energy like natural gas, coal or oil, that could be potentially dangerous to the environment. Furthermore windmills are not composed of dangerous materials that need to be handled with extreme caution when it comes time to dispose of a non-working unit.

Another benefit to the use of windmills and wind as an alternative energy source is that it does not interfere with the working of other sources of energy. One can use solar panels and other sources of energy production simultaneously.

Just as there are benefits to using wind as energy there are also some negative factors to consider prior to investing in this type of alternative energy.

Whereas wind can be prevalent both day and night, wind does not necessarily flow at the same rate of speed all the time. Therefore, the production of electricity would not always remain consistent, and may still require the need of an additional source of energy.

Even though one may think that the time right before a thunder storm may be an ideal window to generate a lot of energy, the aftermath of a thunder storm may cost a windmill owner more in repairs then it would give back via generated electricity. Wind turbines can be damaged or completely destroyed when hit by a heavy storm or severe lightning.

This may sound frivolous, but there have been many instances when the rotating blades of the turbines have proved fatal for birds that happened to hit it.

It is not recommended to place wind turbines, or windmills, near one's home, as wind turbines, on an average, create a sound of about 50-60 decibel. The slower the wind's speed results in more sound. The placement of a turbine should also be considered carefully. For example, if a storm were to roll through and dismantle the unit; one would not want the debris damaging their home.

Another thing to consider when installing a wind mill or

turbine is the aesthetic look of having a large fan or fans on your property. In reality it is a matter of individual perception and not everyone looks at things in the same way.

How does Energy Production Using Wind Energy Compare to Other Sources?

When contemplating alternative energy sources, most commercial and residential consumers often compare and contrast the difference between solar and wind power production. For commercial scale power production used to power the national grid, researchers feel that wind turbines are the solution that is chosen most often. The benefit to wind turbines is that they are efficient and effective, and can be installed in a plethora of locations. Most solar panels are restricted to roof top or field mounting, whereas turbines can be installed far out to sea, and done relatively quickly. Unlike the historic turbine models, updated turbines are very quiet and a large system of turbines can generate 2 megawatts of power - enough to power over 2,000 homes.

On a residential scale wind turbines can be a primary choice, however it is becoming increasingly popular to implement a small wind turbine to compliment a solar panel. A small wind turbine can generate electricity when the sun is not shining and even at night, whereas the solar panels only generate electricity during the day time only if the sun is shining.

Wind turbines do have disadvantages based on their size. They are very location specific and enough 360 degree clearance must be available for them to work correctly. Also large turbines are generally used by the power companies due to their efficiency. Small wind turbines are not efficient for most areas, and are generally recommended to be used in areas of that have an above average amount of wind. Often times these small turbines will require a constant speed of airflow. If you live in a region of turbulent air, meaning the wind constantly changing direction, one may find their turbine to be ineffective, and thus choose to gain their energy from solar panels.

Of course if you don't want to be subject to what nature has to offer on a day to day basis there are always other forms of energy that are not directly impacted in the same manner that wind and solar energy are. That being said, these sources are not renewable; gas, coal. etc.

From a price standpoint the average cost for solar energy is calculated at about 32 cents per kilowatt hour. Wind generated energy is significantly cheaper at a cost of about 10 cents per kilowatt hour. Costs per kilowatt hours are calculated by dividing the total expected cost of a system (modules, inverters, installation etc.) by the expected total energy output.

How Much do you have to Spend to get off the Grid using Home Wind Power?

A recent U.S. Energy Information Administration census shows that on average a U.S. household consumes 908 kilowatt hours (kWh) per month, or 10,896 kWh per year (908 kWh x 12 months). At this rate, the said wind turbines would have to produce approximately 1.24 kilowatts (kW) to account for an entire year's consumption. Living off the grid is possible but will require sizeable upfront costs to purchase and install turbines.

Before making the investment to install wind turbines, make sure the target location meets both the geographical and climate suggestive conditions. Furthermore, to reach suitable wind speeds, a tower will most likely have to be installed. Towers can range anywhere from 30 to 120 feet. To completely live off the grid, special batteries will need to be purchased to store backup energy. These items alone can add several thousand dollars to the total cost of setup.

To further answer the question posed, an example has been presented with a fixed scenario in which one could live off the grid.

The turbine would be expected to have a rotating blade about 15 feet in length. The start-up wind speed needed would be about 7.5 mph. The suggested output would be 538kWh at a wind speed of 12 mph. To generate 908 kWh as indicated earlier, the owner will need either 2 wind turbines, or expected to have around 16 mph wind on a constant basis.

The average cost for one similar turbine is around $4,000 plus installation, batteries, and mounting pole. It would be fair to assume that one may spend around $8,000 - $10,000 to have enough turbine resources to completely live off the grid.

The initial setup cost to living off the grid with wind power may be higher than expected, but with government incentives, one may find the conversion worthwhile. For example, The Residential Renewable Energy Tax Credit will refund 30 percent of the total cost of a turbine that's 100 kWs or less and is purchased before December 31, 2016. Additional state tax credits may also be available.

How Efficiently can Wind Energy be Converted to Electrical Energy?

Believe it or not wind energy is considered to be a form of solar energy, however it is not often times thought of as such. Wind is caused by the heating of the atmosphere in an uneven manner, due to the curvature and rotation of the earth. The wind is continuously altered by the earth's terrain, bodies of water, and density.

The process of converting wind energy into electric energy is the result of using a wind turbine. The wind turbines convert the kinetic energy produced by the wind, into mechanical power. The mechanical power that is created by the wind turbine can be used for many things that involve a rotation like motion. Historically one would see wind turbines being used for pumping water, grinding, or the shear use of veneration or forced air (i.e. a fan). Even though most of these things still occur, wind power is also used to generate electricity.

The wind turbine is a tall rod or cylinder looking pole,

with several horizontal rectangular blades attached to it, usually connected to the center by one point. Picture a large fan. These blades are usually coated with a hardened material. When the wind turns the turbines, the turbine's wheels turn belts, which in turn, rotates a generator. Inside the generator, a coil of copper spins between a couple of magnets. This creates an electrical field, which is converted into DC current. The DC current passes through multiple rectifiers that convert the DC current into AC. AC is the type of current a typical household uses.

There are many types of wind turbines, some are horizontal and some are vertical. The initial design of a wind turbine, closely associates to what one would refer to as a wind mill, it was vertical. Throughout the years mass amounts of research and design were made before the horizontal wind turbine was created.

Wind turbines work in many locations and their output is different depending on the area. Common locations include, large wind farms, residential housing units, commercial and industrial structures, and offshore. Wind farms are capable of converting a large amount of kinetic energy that can be converted to electricity, and eventually power thousands of homes. The best location for wind farms is generally amongst areas where there is a regular flow of wind. If wind turbines are installed where wind may be irregular, this can be hedged by supplying a back-up energy source to account for the smaller amount of energy being generated. Most commonly, solar panels are what are chosen.

It is also possible to create wind farms within a body of water. This is common due to the turbines being unencumbered by buildings, mountains, and other blockages. This process can be very lucrative as it can create a massive amount of energy. The downfall to installing wind turbines on a shoreline or close to a shore line is when the turbines are placed in a row they create a pull which causes a noise disturbance to residents and visitors.

On the residential side of things, wind turbines are capable of generating 50kW of energy per day and can be easily connected to the local grid. Because of this, it is almost effortless to sell back any excess energy to the power company. Not only is wind energy renewable, it is also profitable.

Over the last 9 years the use of wind energy has compounded. In 2013, over seventy five countries are using wind energy on a commercial basis, and these statistics are growing by the year.

What Tax Advantages are there for using Wind Power and what Speeds are Required?

Wind power is a clean, domestic, renewable resource that assists the U.S. in meeting energy, environmental, and economic challenges. Therefore to provide incentive for residential and commercial facilities to covert to wind turbines as an option to generate their electricity, tax credits have been implemented.

Production Tax Credits (PTC) were a part of the Energy Policy Act of 1992 and were intended to promote implementation of wind and bioenergy options. This act provides approximately a 2.2 cent per kilowatt-hour benefit for those who implement wind energy as a source of energy. This credit is applicable every year, through the tenth year. This tax benefit or credit, is only available for wind energy equipment located within the United States, and only if electricity produced is sold to an unrelated party. An added bonus is that any unused credits can be carried forward for twenty years.

On January 2, 2013, Congress temporarily extended the PTC for wind as part of the fiscal cliff bill. The bill also includes an important new provision that allows wind and other eligible renewable energy projects that begin construction in 2013 to qualify for the credit. Previous law required eligible projects to be in-service and operating by the end of the calendar year when the credit was set to expire. Also as a recent update, this legislation allows wind energy sources to qualify for a 30 percent investment tax credit in lieu of the PTC for facilities that begin construction in 2013.

To provide a sense of return a business or residence might get from wind energy investment, the following projections are outlined. If one were to expense $100 million into wind turbines and the necessary installation, the owners would expect a direct deduction from a tax liability of $2,759,400 per year during the first 10 years of operation. Globally the wind turbine initiative would reduce their federal income tax liability by $27,594,000 over the course of 10 years. These calculations were based off the wind turbine matching the capacity of 50 megawatts (MW) and assuming operated at 30% capacity. In turn the turbines would produce 131,400,000 kWh of electricity each year. Again, this is on a larger scale and smaller turbines or single turbines would not produce the same amount of electricity and further not generate the same tax credits.

How Simple is it to Convert a House to Run on Wind Power?

When one is considering converting their home to run on wind power, proper preparation is needed. The consumer needs to be aware that there are an abundance of options out there, and they need to make certain that they are comparing apples to apples, as different set ups are used for commercial facilities versus a residential setup. A normal residential setup involves installing one or more small wind turbines to either fully provide energy, or to supplement your existing energy supply. Home wind turbines need to be of sufficient size so that they produce more energy than they use, this is often a common mistake, and yields a lot of wasted resources.

Initial steps include, establishing whether or not you have sufficient wind in your area to make turbine installation a rewarding option. To help gauge this accurately one may seek professional assistance. After it is determined that there is adequate wind speed in your area, it is then advised that you, contact your local authority to insure there are no special permits or restrictions, that would prohibit the installation of a turbine on your property. The next step would be to find out how much energy you currently consume, to insure the proper size turbine(s) are purchased. Your local or current energy provider can help you interpret your average consumption. Once you have properly determined which turbine(s) to purchase, it is then time to consider whether or not a professional should be hired to complete the installation.

Here is a general overview of what will need to happen to make your system operate:

First you must determine what the voltage of your turbine's alternator is. This information is generally printed or stamped on the outer panels of the unit, and will also be disclosed in the manuals or paperwork that accompanies your turbine. A majority of the residential wind turbine systems output 12-volt DC current, and because of that many users choose to use a battery array or setup. Aside from the voltage determination, you will also need to know what the top output of your generator is in watts. It ranges from 100 to 300 watts. Again you may find this information printed on the housing or in the literature provided.

Next you will need to install a DC-to-AC inverter by running the DC electrical cable from your turbine to the input junction on the inverter. The instructions on how to do this will be included with the inverter. This is where it becomes worthwhile to have professional assistance. The inverter should have a peak throughput which is higher than the maximum output of your turbine. Inverters convert the DC output of the turbine to three-phase 120-volt 60 Hz AC power. This conversion is what makes it possible to use the electricity generated in your home.

You will then need to wire the inverter to your house's main breaker, just as you would with any other wiring conduit in your home. This connection will also need to hook into your electrical meter. After everything is hooked up and active, when adequate wind is present, the turbine will move, thus creating electricity. When your turbine is generating more power than you are using, your electric meter will run backward, thus not only saving you money, but potentially earning you money as well.

Blake Webster

How much Electricity is Produced by Wind Power?

There are many different ways to determine the amount of electricity produced by wind power. The questions is somewhat vague, and varies depending on several factors, namely the size, reliability of the turbine, and the wind speed at the time of measurement.

The amount of energy produced by a turbine.

Typically modern turbines range in size from 660 kilowatts to over 3 megawatts of capacity. They are placed in fairly windy locations with minimum wind speeds in the range of six meters per second (around 13 miles per hour). Wind turbines generally run at 30 to 40 percent capacity, so a 1 MW turbine could produce around 3 million KWh of electricity in a year.

Based on independent research it has been determined that one 1.8 MW wind turbine at an appropriate site (constant and adequate wind) would produce over 391,666 kWh of electricity each month, which is enough to meet the monthly needs of over 1,000 households. In the United Kingdom an average household with 2 parents and 2 children, uses approximately 5500 kWh of energy per year.

Another study concluded that a single 1MW turbine operating at a 45% production rate will generate about 3,900,000 kWh of electricity per year. This would be enough electricity to serve the needs of about 500 households per year.

The energy production of a wind turbine is calculated using a variety of inputs and factors. The wind resource, elevation, temperature range, and turbine power curve. The weather varies day by day and season to season, whereas the power curve is unit specific. Studies that determine wind speed or availability are often expressed as an annual average, but this average does not account for seasonal variation, and generally makes assumptions that wind speeds are normally distributed across the month or throughout the year. This usually skews the accuracy of the assumptions. For example, a turbine may produce 7.4 million kWh per year, but if a majority of the electricity is produced in Jan through May, there will not be enough electricity generated in June through December to meet the demand.

For those of you that would like a more exact calculation there is an advanced method for accurately analyzing wind energy production, which is based on calculus and statistical models. There are entire books written on this, but to provide a brief overview, to calculate the sum of wind energy produced at every instant in the year, one must use specific resource data for that instant as the year progresses. This is very tedious to do by hand, and is often done using advanced software. There are websites and software available that make the job easier and will calculate wind turbine (and solar panel) output at any site in the US using this method. It allows the comparison of different products to see how they will work at your specific location. Some programs also help calculate a payback period analysis as well.

How is Energy Generated from Stored Wind Power?

In general energy that is produced from wind power plants (i.e. a string of wind turbines) is usually immediately fed into power lines where it is used by consumers. As one can imagine wind power plants only generate energy when a steady constant wind flow is present. Due to the fact that the wind does not blow at a constant speed all times, it is expected that wind turbines are not able to generate power every hour of every day, because of this, they are not commonly used as a sole source of power generation. Fortunately, wind power is a clean source of energy and is widely available, and because of this scientists have focused on finding ways to store wind power for later use, especially at times when wind is not present or conducting adequate electricity. Currently, scientists have developed three storage methods, they are battery, compressed air and hydrogen.

Battery

Instead of feeding electricity directly into power lines as mentioned above, energy that is generated from wind turbines can now be used to charge batteries. In essence, the charged batteries hold the electricity, and consumers can then pull from these batteries when there is a lack of wind speed necessary to keep up with the consumption.

Compressed Air

An alternate method for storing wind energy is via compressed air. Compressed air storage is called compressed air energy storage (CAES). The starting point for CAES, begins with the wind turbines generating energy which is then converted to compressed air. The compressed air is then stored either in above ground or below ground tanks. The stored air can then be released through turbines to generate power. The benefit of compressed air storage over batteries, is that hundreds of hours of energy (Compressed air) can be stored, allowing for the ability to provide electricity for hundreds of hours when there is a lack of wind present. This practice has been proven in many case studies both in the US and overseas. There is a wind power facility in Huntorf, Germany that has been using the compressed air storage method since 1978 and one in McIntosh, Alabama that has been using it since 1991.

Hydrogen

Hydrogen is another way in which wind energy can be stored for later use. This involves storing excess wind power in hydrogen fuel cells. Electricity generated from the wind power plant, goes through a process of splitting water into oxygen and hydrogen. The by product, hydrogen is then stored in hydrogen fuel cells and is used when there is a lull in adequate wind speeds, necessary to create energy.

Can Wind Power be Generated for Small Homes with Little Space?

The simple answer is yes. Wind power can be generated for small homes with little space, but it may not be the most effective method, as more research needs to be conducted along with proper installation. The most efficient design is the type of turbine with a simple airplane style propeller that faces the wind. Imagine a large airplane propeller on a stick. That being said, one must have the overhead clearance to allow the propeller to spin with no interference. Also another thing to remember is that wind turbines can be a little noisy, so the closer they are to your residence, the noise byproduct may become a disturbance to your home and your neighborhood. In most cases there are rules or home owners association by laws to prevent this, so a wind turbine may not be the best option for you depending on the area in which you live.

If building codes and bylaws do not restrict construction of a wind machine, and you decide to move forward with putting up a turbine in an area with limited space, the use of a tower or long beam, generally a few stories high may be necessary to provide you with the overhead clearance you would need to allow the propeller to spin properly. If a installing a wind tower on your property is not a viable option, there may be an option for a few home owners to team up and utilize shared space that can adequately house a turbine large enough to power more than one home. If more than one homeowner is willing to participate in a joint venture, since the wind is free, operational costs are nearly zero once a turbine is erected. The only shared cost will be for initial installation, and upkeep as needed. At the end of last year, global capacity was more than 70,000 megawatts. In the United States, a single megawatt is enough electricity to power about 250 homes, if you reside in a larger neighborhood, and convince the local government or home owners association to allow for such construction, the cost over 250 homes would spread thin and provide an opportunity for savings for decades to come. Mass production and technology advances are making turbines cheaper, and many governments offer tax incentives to spur wind-energy development.

How do I Calculate my Power Usage in Order to Install Adequate Wind Generation in my Home?

There are a couple ways that to calculate power usage. In some examples, the calculations can be very complex and for others it may be very easy. As a conceptual overview, one will need to determine the peak load for the power inverter, which is the combination of all loads that might run together. As an example, depending on where you reside, it would not be common for the heat pump and air conditioning to be running together at the same time. In addition, you need to add the starting amps of the biggest electric motor found at your residence or office. Most commonly, the largest motor would be that of your air conditioning unit. If your home does not utilize central air condition, the refrigerator would most likely be the second option, which takes about 4-6 amps to run but 15-20 to start.

A somewhat accurate way to measure consumption would be measure your electric meter reading and then turn on all the appliances that you'd ever use at the same time and let them run for an hour. Following the hour of consumption, take the reading again from your homes meter. Then subtract the end reading from the starting reading, and add 14 amps for your refrigerator. That will give you a maximum kilowatt measure consumed within an hour. You would then need to determine which wind turbine based on your location would generate enough electricity to power your home, per hour. Remember the wind does not blow at all times, so the utilization of a backup source such as solar panel or existing electricity provider may still be necessary.

The second and most common way for one to measure their average energy consumption would be to compare an entire years' worth of electric bills or invoices. By taking the average amount of energy used this would account for warm months where the air conditioning would be in use, as well as the coldest months where the most amount of heat is utilized. Again, this depends on the setup of your home. For example, if you operate your home's heat from an oil tank, without converting your home to a central heating system, a wind turbine may not be an effective way to save money during the colder months. The conversion of heating for your home could be a costly modification, so this should also be taken into consideration.

Generally speaking, before going completely off the grid using alternative energy, one will usually make changes to their home by making it more energy efficient. This might involve using compact florescent bulbs, new energy efficient windows; sometimes appliances are also replaced depending on their age. Extra batteries and inverters used in conjunction with wind turbines and solar panels are also very costly and making your home more energy efficient may be a cheaper option versus having extra batteries or inverters.

In summary the average power usage of Americans is about 1 kilowatt per person. A moderately remodeled energy efficient home could lower this usage to 0.5 kw per person. Before going totally off the grid, it is recommended to try and reach a usage of 0.2 kilowatts per person or better.

What are the Best Home Wind Power Kits?

When in the market for a residential wind turbine, there are many options to choose from. There are different shapes and sizes and each has a different optimal level of use. The first step is to do your homework, to understand how much energy your home consumes, and how much wind your geographical area produces on average. Once you have determined all of the essential factors it is then time to pick out your turbine.

Per the general consensus, below we have compiled a list of the top four micro turbines.

Southwest Windpower Skystream 3.7

This turbine is considered to be a "plug and play" model. Everything required such as an inverter and controls are already built in. It is quiet, and produces clean electricity in even the smallest amount of wind speed.

Cost: Approximately $5399 (not including tower and installation materials)

Rated Capacity: 1.9 kW continuous output, 2.6 kW peak
Startup Windspeed: 8mph

Rotor: 12 feet (3.72 m); 50-325 RPM

Interconnection: Utility connected or battery charging

Alternator: Gearless, permanent magnet brushless

Voltage Output: 240 VAC (Optional 208 VAC)

Estimated Energy Production: 400 kWh/month @ 12 MPH (5.4 m/s)

Southwest Windpower AIR X

The AIR X is supposedly the world's number one selling small wind turbine. This turbine incorporates a microprocessor based technology that yields the ultimate performance. High performance measures include, improved battery charging capability, greater reliability and the reduction of "flutter" noise from the machine.

This turbine has been ideally designed for powering small appliances in off-grid installations, remote communications facilities, marine applications, and communities in the developing world.

Cost: $600

Rated Capacity: 400 watts

Startup Wind speed: 8mph

Rotor: 46 inches (1.14 m)

Interconnection: Battery charging

Voltage Output: 12, 24, 48 VDC

Estimated Energy Production: 288 kWh/month @ 12 MPH (5.4 m/s

Southwest Windpower Whisper 500

This unit can produce enough energy to power a small to moderately sized home. Roughly a home about the size of 1,000 to 1,400 square feet. The unit houses a fiberglass reinforced blade and includes a specialized and preparatory governor designed for quiet operations in high winds. This turbine is unique in the sense that it has over speed protection which allows the blades to angle differently without cutting power output.

Cost: $7,095

Rated Capacity: 3kw

Startup Wind speed: 7.5mph

Rotor: 15 feet (4.6 m)

Interconnection: Utility connected or battery charging

Voltage Output: 24, 32, 48 VDC or 240 VAC

Estimated Energy Production: 500 KWh/month @12.5mph

Bergey Excel

The Bergey Excel is perfect for any homeowner looking to "go green". This turbine is designed for high reliability, low maintenance, and automatic operation in adverse weather conditions. You can purchase this turbine kit in one of two configurations: battery charging or grid-tied.

When this unit is connected to the grid, the BWC EXCEL can provide enough electricity for the average home. Wind Speeds required for such production are considered "moderate".

This unit comes with a 5 year warranty.

Cost: $21,900-$27,900

Rated Capacity: 10kw

Startup Wind speed: 7.5 mph

Rotor: 22 feet (6.7 m)

Interconnection: Utility connected or battery charging

Voltage Output: 48 VDC or 120, 240 VAC

Estimated Energy Production: 1500 KWh/month @12.5mph

Just as a disclosure for this overview, all prices are that of the MSRP. All Prices change over time and they could be higher or lower depending on the outlet you are shopping.

How much Energy would a
Small Wind Turbine Generate?

There are many different factors that go into the calculation of how much energy a small wind turbine can generate. Factors include, wind speed, size of turbine, height of turbine from the ground, turbine efficiencies, and the inclusion or exclusion over speed governors.

The ability to generate electricity is measured in watts. Watts are very small units, so the terms kilowatt (kW, 1,000 watts), megawatt (MW, 1 million watts), and gigawatt (GW, 1 billion watts) are most commonly used to describe the capacity of generating units like wind turbines or other power plants.

Generally, electricity production and consumption are measured in kilowatt-hours (kWh). A kilowatt-hour means one kilowatt (1,000 watts) of electricity produced or consumed for one hour. For example, one generic 50-watt light bulb left on for 20 hours consumes one kilowatt-hour of electricity (50 watts x 20 hours = 1,000 watt-hours = 1 kilowatt-hour).

As mentioned earlier, the output of a wind turbine id dependent on the turbine's size and the wind's speed through the rotor. Most of the turbines manufactured today have power ratings that range from the smallest at 250 watts to some of the largest at 5 megawatts (MW).

To provide you with an example a 10 kilowatt wind turbine can generate about 10,000 kWh annually at a location with wind speeds averaging 12 miles per hour. This is approximately enough electricity to power a typical household. On a smaller scale, a 5-MW turbine can produce more than 15 million kWh in a year. This is approximately enough electricity to power more than 1, 400 households. The average U.S. household consumes about 10,000 kWh of electricity each year.

Again, there are variable factors that go into the calculations. For example, wind speed is a critical element in projecting turbine performance. An average calculation of wind speed can be measured through a wind resource assessment prior to construction. Generally, an annual average wind speed of at least four meters per second (m/s) (9 mph) is necessary for small wind electric turbines to power a small home. Utility-scale wind power plants require minimum average wind speeds of 6 m/s (13 mph).

The power available in the wind is directly correlated to the cube of its speed. This means by doubling the wind speed one would expect to see an increase in the available power output, by a factor of eight. Thus, a turbine operating on location with an average wind speed of 12 mph could generate about one-third more electricity than one at an 11-mph site, because the cube of 12 (1,768) is one-third larger than the cube of 11 (1,331). What seems like a small difference in wind speed can mean a large difference in available energy and in electricity produced, therefore, a large difference in the cost of the electricity generated.

How do I Measure the Amount of Energy Produced by a Home Wind Turbine?

There are many variables that affect the amount of power generated by a home wind turbine. Consumers are advised to avoid general ratings and meticulously study the power generating capacity of a wind turbine at the potential location.

Most turbines rate their output production in kilowatts (kW). The rating is can be compared to a cars horsepower measure. This is basically a measure of size, which is larger. In the analysis of a car, the horsepower measure doesn't indicate the fuel efficiency, top speed, driving conditions, or even driver experience. Most everyone has owned a car, so during the test drive you can usually detect a difference in a cars horse power, however most turbine consumers are generally first time buyers and have no measure of comparison.

Most utility bills distributed within the United States are measured in kilowatt-hours (kWh). (i.e. power usage multiplied by time). To help illustrate this concept, a 100-watt light bulb in use for 10 hours consumes one kWh. Industry research indicates that a 10 kW wind turbine system will generate about 10,000 kWh per year which equals the average amount of consumption for a normal US household. That being said, the real output will be higher or significantly lower, depending on the variable factors at the site of installation. In summary the turbine puts out a maximum of 10 kW under perfect conditions, so it could theoretically generate 10 kW for 24 hours a day 365 days a year, or 87,600 kW per year. As we know there are never perfect conditions, so this measure will vary, however if you have the desire to get an exact measure, one can calculate the accurate power output of a wind turbine in watts by multiplying the mechanical efficiency, by the wind speed, air density, and rotor blade length.

If you have already invested in a wind turbine and are seeking an accurate measure of output, you can easily cross reference your old electrical bills prior to installing the turbine. This must be done on a month to month comparative basis in order to account for seasonal factors. For instance one would not compare December's bill with no turbine, to June's bill with a turbine. In order to get a somewhat accurate calculation you would generally start with the higher months bill before the turbine was installed, and then subtract out the most recent comparative months bill (with the turbine in use). This calculation will only work if you are not completely off the grid, as the difference in usage will equal the amount of energy produced by the turbine.

If you are seeking the production measure of a turbine to determine your payback period, again there are many variables involved. The length of the payback period depends on the turbine, the quality of wind at the installation site, prevailing electricity rates, and available financing and incentives. Depending on these and other factors, the time it takes to fully recover the cost of a small wind turbine can take anywhere from 6 to 30 years.

What is a Grid Tie-in Home Wind Generator?

To help one determine what a grid based wind generation system is, and a non-based generation system is the two will be compared for a full overview.

What is considered being "On the Grid"?

A home or office that is currently connected to a locally provided power source is considered "on the grid." You will know you are on the grid because you will receive a monthly bill for your energy consumption. If you are "on the grid" using a wind turbine system, this would generally mean that you are supplementing your providers electricity with power from your wind turbine when the unit is running. If there are inadequate periods of wind, then the contracted energy provider will provide the necessary energy needed for your home or office's consumption. You will then be billed for electricity used. To the contrast, when your installed turbine generates more electricity than your home uses, your meter can actually spin backwards, at which time you would be selling electricity back to your electric provider.

An on-grid system can be worthwhile if the following

conditions are met:

- You live in an area with an average annual wind speed of at least 10 mph (4.5m/s)
- Contracted electricity is expensive in your area. Usually higher in metropolitan areas.
- The requirements for connecting your turbine to your existing home's electrical setup is not exuberantly expensive
- There are good incentives for the sale of excess electricity for the purchase of wind turbines

What is considered being "Off the Grid"?

Homes or offices that are not connected to a local utility supplier are known as "off the grid" households. Generally if your home or office is considered off the grid, one will utilize a hybrid system that combines the use of solar paneling and wind turbines as a mean of producing electricity. This type of setup would provide minimal interruptions as each unit, whether it is a solar panel or wind turbine, will complement each other's periods of inefficiency. In many parts of the US, wind speeds are low in the summer when the sun shines brightest and are relatively high in the winter when less sunlight is available. In case of emergency, off-grid systems normally have an engine or gas generator on hand, that can be easily tied in to the home or office setup as well.

An "off the grid" system may be practical under the following conditions:

- You live in an area with an average annual wind speed of at least 9 mph (4.0m/s)
- A normal electricity provider is not available in your area or can only be made through an expensive extension. This is often found in very remote locations.

You would like to gain energy independence from the utility company.

How Long will it Take to Recoup my Investment?

Just like many of the other discussions about wind turbines and their effectiveness, the amount of time that it takes to recoup ones investment varies, and is based on a number of factors. Factors include size, location, geographic wind studies, and the size of one's home and their average energy consumption.

For this example, the case study includes a 6 kilowatt system that is made up of 15 turbines, produced by a company called AeroVironment. The cost for said system retails for about $35,000 and equates to about $5-$7 per watt, which includes installation and all equipment. It is estimated that with average to good wind conditions, this system could possibly generate about $1,000 worth of electricity per year. Again, energy rates vary depending on your geographic location. Based on the assumptions above, it is estimated that the said investment will take 35 years to breakeven. It is a fair assumption to say that under normal circumstances, very few families reside in their home for 35 years. The average is more like 15 years, if not less. Prior to investing in a wind powered alternate energy source, a breakeven analysis would need to match a 10 year payback period to make a turbine investment worthwhile.

To provide another case study or example of the time it takes to recoup the investment of a wind turbine, the WT6500 model manufactured by Windtrocis can be analyzed.

The WT6500 is similar to traditional wind turbines, which can be mounted to the roof of one's home. Similar to other comparable turbines, any unused energy it generates can be sold to the local electricity provider for a credit. This idea is basically like spinning the electric meter backwards.

In the geographic location of Yonkers, New York it is estimated that the said turbine would produce 1,155 kWh per year at a 12-mph average wind speed. Another thing to consider is that the turbine generated its highest rating at an installed height of 164 feet. The turbine might tower over the home more than one might like.

In this test case, 15 months after installation, the turbine had only produced 4 kWh worth of energy which was hardly enough only to power a 12,000 btu window air conditioner for an afternoon. Supposedly this unit would require at least 6 mph of wind speed to power the unit's inverter which is required for the unit to generate a positive return to the residence.

At the rate the WT6500 is producing electricity, it has been concluded that it would take hundreds of years for the product to pay for itself.

A wind turbine typically lowers a personal residential electric bill by 50% to 90%. If the subject residence is powered completely by electricity and not oil, or other natural gas, based on some of the best conditions, one would expect to see their average electricity bill at $20 per month. It is possible for one to install a turbine and have 100% of their electricity bill disappear, but again the amount of money a small wind turbine saves you in the long run will depend upon its cost, the amount of electricity you use, the wind speed at your location and many other variable factors.

About the Author

Blake Webster is a web and multimedia developer, digital product developer, web publisher, search engine optimization consultant, internet marketer, photographer, published author, environmentalist and publisher of the online magazine Greener Living Today ®.

He has taught web development and consulted businesses in the San Francisco Bay area since 1996.

He also works with authors by promoting their work online, laying out manuscripts for CreateSpace and converting manuscripts for Amazon Kindle.

In addition Blake offers workshops for WordPress, social media, social media SEO and Kindle marketing.

Learn more by visiting the following web sites:

www.mediadesignservices.com

www.socialwebmediatraining.com

www.greenerlivingtoday.com

www.ingramcontent.com/pod-product-compliance
Lightning Source LLC
Chambersburg PA
CBHW070620290526
45790CB00002B/944